My First Book about the Alphabet of Reptiles

Amazing Animal Books Children's Picture Books

By Molly Davidson

Mendon Cottage Books

JD-Biz Publishing

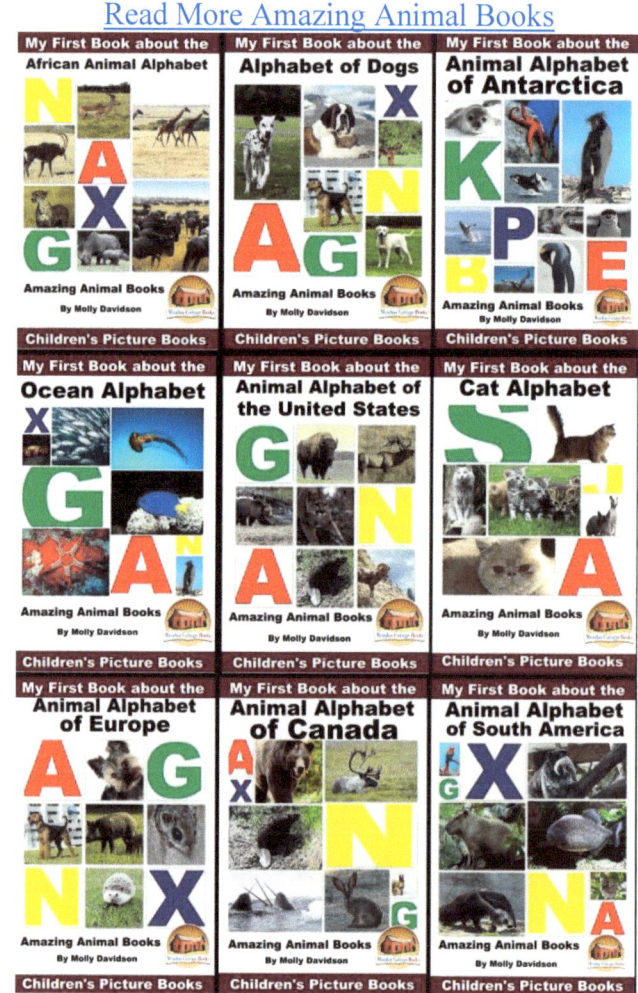

Introduction

All reptiles have scales or a hard shell to protect themselves.

They lay eggs, and are cold blooded, which means they need to get heat from the outside, like the sun, to keep warm.

 is for an Alligator.

Alligators live in the southern United States and only a few still live in China.

They are one of the fastest large reptiles on land, running up to 15 mph.

 is for a Bearded Dragon.

Wild bearded dragons are found in Australia.

They can grow to be 24 inches long, but most of that is their long tail.

They eat crickets, worms, and insects.

C is for a Chameleon.

Chameleons live in the jungles and deserts of Africa, Asia, and southern Europe.

Some species of chameleon are able to change their skin color so they can camouflage with their environment.

D is for a Dakosaurus.

Dakosaurus, like all dinosaurs, were reptiles, but they have been extinct for millions of years.

They had very sharp teeth, which were used to kill whales and other large ocean animals.

 is for an Eastern Coral Snake.

John © <u>Wikimedia Commons</u>

Eastern Coral snakes are venomous snakes that live around the coasts of the south east U.S.

When they are threatened they curl their tail so the predator doesn't know which end is the head.

 **is for a False Gharial.**

They live in rivers, swamps, and lakes in Malaysia and Indonesia.

False gharials are a saltwater crocodile with a long, skinny snout.

G is for a Gila Monster.

The Gila monster is a venomous lizard that lives in Mexico and the southern U.S.

They have long sharp claws which they use for digging burrows in the dirt, which is where they spend most of their time.

 **is for a Horned Lizard.**

The horned lizard lives in the deserts of central North America.

Some horned lizard species shoot blood from the corners of their eyes when they are attacked.

I is for an Iguana.

Iguanas are a large lizard that lives in the jungles of the Caribbean, and Central and South America.

They like to stay high in the trees, usually over water, so they can escape predators by jumping out of tree into the water below.

J

is for a Japanese Skink.

Japanese skinks have a blue tail that they use to attract predators, and then it breaks off so they can escape, a new tail will shortly grow back.

K is for a Komodo Dragon.

Komodo dragons are the largest lizards in the World, and are only found in Indonesia.

They are very aggressive and kill prey much larger than themselves, like pigs, water buffalo, goats, deer, and horses. .

L is for a Leopard Gecko.

They live in the deserts of Asia, Pakistan, and northern India.

Leopard geckos will shed their skin about once a month, which they then eat!

They have about 100 teeth.

M is for a Mamba.

Mambas are a venomous snake that lives only in Africa.

They are the fastest land snake, and can scurry away from danger as fast as 12 mph.

Mothers will lay 6 - 25 eggs in a wet burrow, in about 3 months the babies will hatch.

 **is for a New Guinea Crocodile.**

New Guinea crocodiles are only found in New Guinea.

They are different from other crocodiles because they rarely come out of the water during the day; usually it is only at night.

Some grow to be as long as 11 1/2 feet.

O is for an Ornithischia Stegosaur.

Fossils of the ornithischia stegosaur have been found in the United States and Portugal.

Some were over 30 feet in length!

They had between 17 - 22 separate spikes running down their spine.

P is for a Python.

Pythons are some of the largest, nonvenomous snakes in the world.

They can grow to be over 30 feet long, and live in Asia, Africa, and Australia.

They live for about 25 - 35 years in the wild.

R is for a Radiated Tortoise.

Radiated tortoises live in the bushy forests and grass lands of Madagascar.

They are an endangered animal, due to habitat loss.

Tortoises live more than 80 years on average.

S is for a Sea Turtle.

Sea turtles are found in all the World's oceans, except in the Arctic Circle, it is too cold.

They will swim for hundreds and thousands of miles to lay their eggs on the same beach, almost the same spot, every single year.

T is for a Tyrannosaurus.

Tyrannosaurus, which is the Latin word for king, have had their fossils found all over North America.

T is also for a Tuatara.

The almost extinct tuatara is a lizard found only on the islands of New Zealand.

They have a third eye on the top of their head.

Many tuatara live for over 100 years.

U

is for a Uromastyx Loricata.

![Uromastyx loricata lizard]

Omid Mozaffari © <u>Wikimedia Commons</u>

Uromastyx loricata is the scientific name for a spiny tailed lizard.

They can be found living in Iraq, Iran, and Kuwait.

 **is for a Viper.**

Vipers have two large fangs that they use to kill and sometimes inject venom into their prey.

These very dangerous snakes live all over the World, except in Australia and Antarctica.

They are mostly active at night, and usually ambush their prey.

W  is for Water Dragon.

Water dragons are found in the jungles and forests of Asia and Australia.

They have sharp claws and strong legs which help them climb trees.

They spend lots of their time swimming and around water.

 **is for a Xenopeltidae.**

![Bernard DUPONT © Wikimedia Commons]

Bernard DUPONT © <u>Wikimedia Commons</u>

Xenopeltidae snakes have iridescent scales and live in Southeast Asia.

They can grow to be as long as 4 feet!

 **is for a Yellow Monitor.**

The yellow monitor, also called the golden lizard, lives in Asia.

Their bodies are about the same length as their tail, total they measure a little more than 3 feet long.

 **is for a Zhou's Box Turtle.**

Zhou's box turtles are only found in China.

There are very few left in the wild, most are killed and sold as a food delicacy in Chinese markets.

Conclusion

We hope you have enjoyed reading about some amazing reptiles.

Here is one more fact; there are over 8,000 species of reptile alive today.

Our books are available at

1. Amazon.com

2. Barnes and Noble

3. Itunes

4. Kobo

5. Smashwords

6. Google Play Books

Download Free Books!
http://MendonCottageBooks.com

Publisher

JD-Biz Corp

P O Box 374

Mendon, Utah 84325

http://www.jd-biz.com/

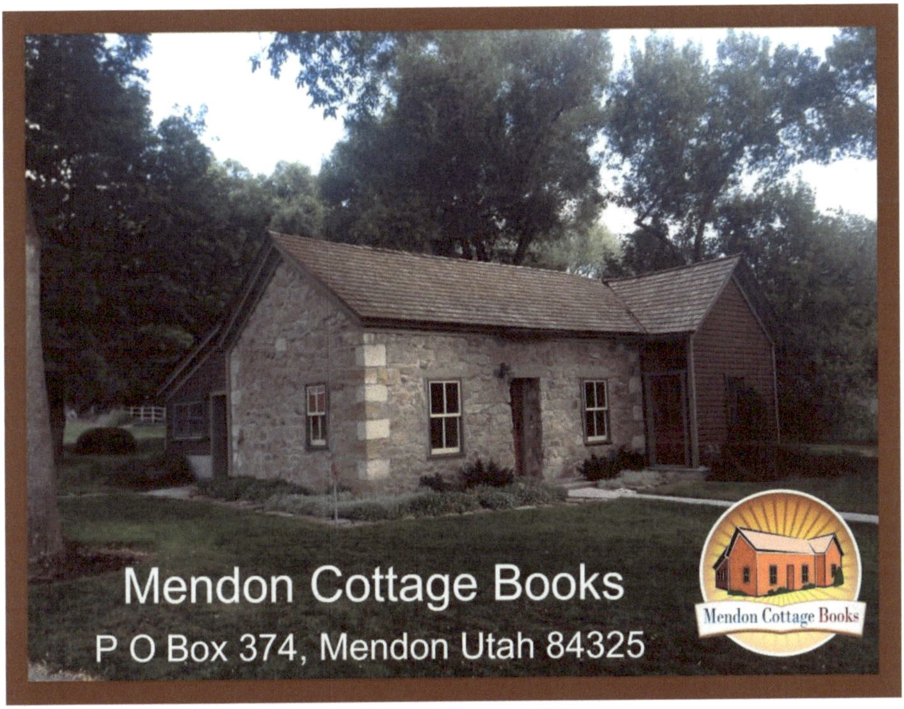

Mendon Cottage Books

P O Box 374, Mendon Utah 84325

www.ingramcontent.com/pod-product-compliance
Lightning Source LLC
Chambersburg PA
CBHW050903290526
45792CB00002B/679